GUINNESS WORLD RECORDS

for Girls

meadowside
CHILDREN'S BOOKS

2004 Meadowside Children's Books
Fleet Street, London
www.meadowsidebooks.com

British Library Cataloguing-in-Publication data is available from the British Library.

ISBN: 1-904511-56-2

Compiled by:
Lorna Ainger, Jon Richards, Ben Ruocco, Ed Simkins and Siân Williams.

For Guinness World Records:
Jerramy Fine, Claire Folkard, Craig Glenday, Betty Halvagi and Keely Hopkins

Picture acknowledgements
The publishers would like to thank the following for their kind permission to reproduce the photographs:

Alamy: Cosmo Condina 53m
Album: Paramount/20th Century Fox 37
Corbis: Pete Saloutos 62b
Courtesy Cunard: 46
Digital Vision: 6t, 6-7, 11b, 12, 13r, 14-15, 18m, 21t, 23t, 23b, 26t, 27t, 27b, 28b, 29l, 29t, 30br, 38bl, 40l, 48tl, 50t, 50b, 51bl, 52tl, 52bl, 52br, 53tl, 53tr, 53m, 55b
EPA/PA Photos: 63bl
Getty Images: AFP 17, 58r; Evan Agostini 57; Odd Andersen 34; Graham Barclay 28t; David Cheskin 59b; Anthony Harvey 60l; Munawar Hosain 16; Hulton 36t; Keystone 43tr; Bryn Lennon 35; John Li 25; Lawrence Lucier 24; Frank Micelotta 9; NBC 45; Graeme Robertson 40m, 41b; Pascal Le Segretain 56, 58r; Steve Taylor 19b; David Westing 44; Kevin Winter 8
Courtesy of Guinness World Records: 7t, 7m, 10, 11t, 13l, 14r, 15t, 18l, 20, 21b, 22, 26b, 30t, 31l, 31tr, 32–33 all, 36br, 39l, 39r, 42br, 43tl, 43bl, 47t, 48b, 49t, 51br, 54, 55t, 60r, 61tr, 61b
Courtesy Gulfstream Aerospace Corporation 47bl
Courtesy MTV Europe 40bl
PA Photos: Tim Ockenden 53m
Rex Features: Clive Dixon 19t
Ross Parry Picture agency: 38tr

Printed in United Arab Emirates

10 9 8 7 6 5 4 3 2 1

contents

If you want to get your name in the record books, turn to page 64 and find out how

Girls!

Welcome to your very own book of Guinness World Records!

ROBODOG

This cute little guy is Sony's AIBO, the world's fastest selling entertainment robot (AIBO means 'pal' in Japanese). Although he costs $2,066 (£1,132), the first 3,000 sold out in just 20 minutes! This robo-puppy can recognize its own name and surroundings, and can even learn to perform tricks.

Have you ever dreamed about being the best in the world at something? A glamorous actress, a savvy business woman or a gold medal athlete? Or maybe you just appreciate glamorous things, like diamond tiaras and high-heeled shoes!

If so, this is the book for you! It's filled with outlandish animals, lavish locations and fabulous facts on your favourite record-breaking celebs... you won't be able to put it down! And if you're inspired to shoot for the stars and break a record yourself, we've included everything that you need to know on page 64.

ROMANTIC RODENT

Sooty from South Wales holds the record for the most valentines sent to a guinea pig. He was sent the cards after he managed to father 43 babies by 24 partners in a single night! He received 206 cards – some from as far away as New Zealand.

So dive in and enjoy these fabulous Guinness World Records – all chosen just for you!

from
The Girls
at GWR
x

MOST VALUABLE JEWEL

This rather tasty diamond went for an amazing SF20 million (£8.4 million) when it was sold in auction at Sotheby's, Geneva, on 17 May 1995. This 100.10-carat rock might be a little too big for a ring, but what girl wouldn't love it dangling round her neck!?

HIGH JUMPERS

Dolphins are the Olympic gold medallists of the watery world. Bottlenose dolphins can jump as high as 7.9 m – more than three times the human high jump record, which is just 2.45 m. That's like you leaping over a minibus!

amazing

ENORMOUS ENTERTAINERS

The biggest land beast is the African elephant. The heaviest can weigh up to eight tonnes – as much as three cars! Their Asian cousins may not be as heavy but they make up for it in musical talent – 12 elephants from Thailand have formed the largest animal orchestra. They even have their own CD!

DID YOU KNOW?
SLOWEST MAMMAL

With an average ground speed of just 1.8 m per minute, the three-toed sloth of South America is one animal that's not in a hurry to get anywhere.

QUIZ TIME Should you ever happen to find yourself cruising up the Yangtze river, keep an eye out for the world's rarest marine mammal, the river dolphin. But which country would you be travelling through?

DID YOU KNOW? FASTEST MAMMAL

Don't blink or you might miss the cheetah! This cruising cat can sprint to speeds of 100 km/h in short spurts – and can accelerate faster than a sports car!

OLD TIMER

Shown here cuddling his very own Guinness World Records certificate is Cheeta the chimpanzee. Star of many Tarzan films, at 73 years old he's the world's oldest primate – he even managed to outlive his first owner!

animals

Grab your camera and join our glamorous Guinness World Records safari. You'll come face to face with the world's most incredible creatures and rub shoulders with the stars of the animal kingdom!

TREMENDOUS TORTOISE!

Meet Goliath – he's the world's largest tortoise. At his biggest, the slow-mover from the Galapagos Islands was 135.8 cm long and 102 cm wide, and weighed a toe-crushing 417 kg!

HOW DO YOU MEASURE UP?

The long jump record holder of the animal kingdom is the kangaroo, which can leap a distance of 12.8 m. Using a tape measure, see how far you can jump. Can you get anywhere near this marvellous marsupial?

QUIZ TIME Sadly, the Iberian Lynx of Spain and Portugal is the world's most endangered wild cat. How many do you think are left in the world? a) 3 b) 104 c) 600

BRiTNEY spears

BRiTNEY facts

- Before she reached the age of 20, Britney had not only dated Justin Timberlake, but she had sold 37 million records around the world, making her the planet's biggest selling teenage artist.
- Her album Oops, I Did It Again is the fastest-selling album for a female artist.
- In 2000, Britney earned about £3,000 every hour of the day and night! Not bad for a teenager!

DID YOU KNOW?

HITCHED IN LAS VEGAS

Britney got married in 2004... but only for 55 hours. Still, that's nowhere near the record for the shortest marriage – actress Eva Bartok left her third husband at the wedding!

NAME: Britney Spears
DATE OF BIRTH: 2 December 1981
PLACE OF BIRTH: Louisiana, USA
OCCUPATION: Singer, movie star

NAME: Madonna Louise Veronica Ciccone (and now Mrs Guy Ritchie)

DATE OF BIRTH: 16 August 1958

PLACE OF BIRTH: Michigan, USA

OCCUPATION: Singer, movie star, children's author

DID YOU KNOW?

MULTI-TALENTED MUM

Madonna has also tried her hand at acting (in the film Evita she had more costume changes than any character in movie history) and recently wrote several children's story books.

MADONNA facts

- Madonna holds the record for the most top 40 singles by a female artist. She broke the record in 2002 when her James Bond single Die Another Day entered the charts. In total she's had 34 top ten hits in the US and 48 top ten hits in the UK.
- This mother of two is also the world's most successful female solo artist, having sold a staggering 120 million albums and 40 million singles.

DID YOU KNOW?

HEAVIEST GOLD RING

The Najmat Taiba ('Star of Taiba') ring would be tricky to wear, but boy would it sparkle! It measures 70 cm across and weighs more than 60 kg!

Bling

They say that diamonds are a girl's best friend. Well, here are a few stones that wil really rock your world!

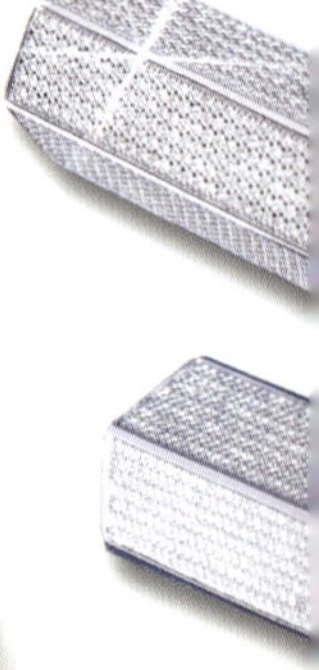

WORLD'S BIGGEST DIAMOND

Can you believe that the world's biggest diamond was nearly ignored? It's true! The man who discovered it, Frederick Wells, thought it was a chunk of glass put in the wall of a mine as a practical joke. Fortunately for him, he took a closer look and unearthed a monster gem. It was cut into over 100 pieces, the largest of which sits at the head of the royal sceptre in the British crown jewels.

DIAMOND ROBBERY

Over £62 million of diamonds were stolen from the Antwerp Diamond Centre in Belgium in February 2003. The alarms didn't go off, and no-one knows how the robbers did it!

QUIZ TIME The highest price paid for a single emerald is \$2,126,646 (£1,320,488) for a 19.77-carat jewel at Sotheby's, Geneva, Switzerland, on 2 April 1987. What colour are emeralds?

bling

GORGEOUS GEMS

A girl simply cannot have enough jewellery these days. And if you're shopping for something that sparkles, you must insist on the best. France's Queen Marie Antoinette had style – she wore a pearl necklace that sold for $1.5 million (£910,313) in 1999. Or perhaps you'd prefer the world's most valuable ruby, which sold for a cool $4.6 million (£2.9 million)? Whichever you choose, you'll have to keep it in the world's most valuable jewellery box – a steal at $189,000 (£127,651)!

MOST VALUABLE JEWEL

This rather tasty diamond went for an amazing SF20 million (£8.4 million) when it was sold in auction at Sotheby's, Geneva, on 17 May 1995. This 100.10-carat rock might be a little too big for a ring, but what girl wouldn't love it dangling round her neck!?

MOST EXPENSIVE JEWELLED PEN

When a girl goes shopping, she must sign her cheques with something that really makes a statement. Well, what better way to do that than with this sparkling pen? Covered in 5,168 diamonds and rubies, it costs a mere £169,000.

QUIZ TIME The world's largest cultured pearl has a diameter of 40 mm and weighs 27.65 g. But which sea creature produces pearls?

bouncing

NOTEWORTHY NIPPERS

Some babies are destined for stardom. Take little Leroy Overacker – at the age of just six months, he became the youngest baby to receive star billing in a movie when he appeared in A Bedtime Story... before he could even talk! And if you think that's impressive, you'll be amazed by baby George Hanover – he was knighted as Sir George at the age of just 29 days! (He grew up to be King George IV.)

These cute little bundles of joy just couldn't wait to start breaking records. Some of them got their names in the record books the moment they were born!

QUIZ TIME Bobbie McCaughey holds the record for giving birth to the most babies at one time. How many did she give birth to on 19 November 1997? a) 7 b) 12 c) 23

DID YOU KNOW?
SHORT AND SWEET

The world's shortest newborn baby was Nisa Juarez, who measured just 24 cm at birth. Little Nisa was born 108 days premature and weighed just 320 g. (11.3 oz)

DOUBLE TROUBLE
Check out these charmful armfuls! Lucky mum JP Haskin of Arkansas, USA, gave birth to twins whose combined weight was 12.6 kg (27lb 12oz) ... making them the world's heaviest twins at birth!

TINY TRIPLETS

Can you believe that this terrific trio weighed less than 1.4 kg (3lb 7oz) in total when they were born!? Peyton, Jackson and Blake Coffey, the world's lightest triplets, were delivered on 30 November 1998, and spent over three months in hospital. But as you can see, they've grown up fit and healthy.

babies

DID YOU KNOW?
PRAM PUSHING

How's this for pushing power? Mal Grimmet from Australia pushed his baby daughter Natalie in a pram over 10 km in just 34 minutes and 26 seconds.

FULL-SIZE FAMILY

69 The number of children born to the wife of Russian peasant Feodor Vassilyev in the 18th century
27 Her total number of pregnancies
16 Sets of twins
7 Sets triplets
4 Sets of quadruplets

QUIZ TIME True or false? Anna Bates gave birth to world's heaviest baby which weighed more than a bowling ball.

at the

Ahhh, this is the life. Sunbathing on the beach, a cold drink in your hand, listening to the waves crash on the shore. Life doesn't get much better than this...

DID YOU KNOW?

ON THE CREST OF A WAVE

Pam Burridge from Australia is one woman who knows how to ride the waves. This surfer earned a cool $296,875 (£160,690) in the 1998 season alone.

PARADISE ISLAND

Dreaming of an enchanted, secluded beach? Then book a sailing boat to Fraser Island, off the coast of Australia. At 120 Km long, it's the world's largest desert island... so you'll have plenty of space all to yourself!

QUIZ TIME Which country holds the record for eating the most ice cream?
a) Greenland b) Mongolia c) Australia

beach

LARGEST BEACH TOWEL
Perfect for a beach party, this huge towel measures 9.4 m by 14.46 m. The only problem is finding a beach with enough space!

BATHING BEAUTY

You'll want to protect your baby blue eyes from the scorching sun with a cool pair of stylish shades. So what better to wear than the most popular sunglasses in the world? Ray-bans have been around since the 1950s but they're still as trendy as ever. The perfect match for your designer shades is obviously the world's most expensive swimwear. Anna Cole of California created a diamond and pearl-encrusted swimsuit that sells for $12,000 (£8,000). In this outfit, you'll be the most envied girl on the beach!

HOW DO YOU MEASURE UP?

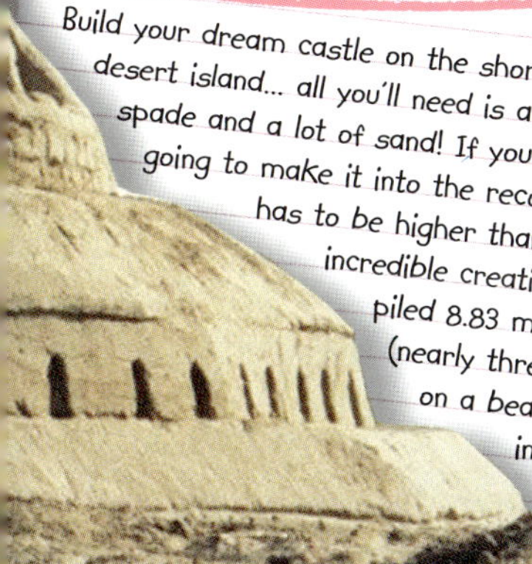

Build your dream castle on the shore of your desert island... all you'll need is a bucket and spade and a lot of sand! If your sandcastle's going to make it into the record books, it has to be higher than this incredible creation. It was piled 8.83 metres high (nearly three storeys!) on a beach in Finland in 2000.

DID YOU KNOW?
LARGEST PLEASURE BEACH

Virginia Beach, USA, is the place to go for a holiday with that little bit extra. It has over 60 km of beautiful sands with hundreds of ocean-front hotels, shops, spas and restaurants.

QUIZ TIME Fuatai Solo can climb a 9-m coconut tree in .88 seconds. At this speed, how fast could he climb the Empire State building?

JULIA facts

- Julia must have the golden touch. She's starred in 31 movies since 1987 and these films took over \$2.5 billion (£1.3 billion) making her the actress with highest box-office gross.
- She shot to fame in the late eighties and early nineties, in movies such as Flatliners and perhaps her most famous film, Pretty Woman.
- Along with Cameron Diaz, she holds the record for the highest salary for a movie actress, taking \$20 million to act in both Erin Brockovich and The Mexican.

JULIA roberts

NAME: Julie Fiona Roberts
DATE OF BIRTH: 28 October 1967
PLACE OF BIRTH: Smyrna, Georgia, USA
OCCUPATION: Actress

CAMERON diaz

NAME: Cameron Michelle Diaz

DATE OF BIRTH: 30 August 1972

PLACE OF BIRTH: San Diego, California, USA

OCCUPATION: Model, actress

CAMERON facts

- Alongside Julia Roberts, Cameron holds the record for the highest salary for an actress. She was paid a cool $20 million for appearing in Charlie's Angels: Full Throttle.

- However, she started out as a model, leaving home at the tender age of 15 to work in Japan for the Elite Model Agency. She spent five years as a model before her big movie break in The Mask.

DID YOU KNOW?

FORMER HIGH ROLLER

Until recently, Cam was the world's highest earning actress of all time. However, she's just been beaten into second place by Jennifer Aniston who earned $35 million (£20.8 million) in 2002.

party time

How's this for a party game? 4,160 people took part in the largest game of Twister at the University of Massachusetts on 13 June 1987!

Girls just wanna have fun, so throw on your party clothes, grab a few friends and hit the dancefloor!

HOW DO YOU MEASURE UP?

Try breaking the record for the world's biggest sleepover party. First you need a very big place to fit all your guests – you'll need more than 1,045 to break the record. And you'll have to make sure that everybody's wearing pyjamas and has their own sleeping bag.

DID YOU KNOW?

LONGEST DANCE PARTY

Do you like to dance til dawn? Well, see if you can beat the record set on 29 July 2003 when 41 dancers completed a dance marathon lasting 52 hr 3 min – better wear your comfy shoes!

QUIZ TIME One of the world's biggest millennium parties took place in New York City, where three million people gathered to see in the New Year. But which two other cities threw record-breaking parties?

HAVING A BALL

If you're throwing the world's biggest party, you'll want the world's largest disco ball to make your evening really sparkle! American party boy Derek Dyer built this giant mirrorball measuring 3 m in diameter and weighing an amazing 450 kg. Get this spinning and you'll won't be able to drag your friends off the dancefloor!

PARTY POPPERS

Start your party with a bang! That's what they did in London on 31 December 1999, on the eve of the new millennium. Over 5 million people turned up to watch as 30 tonnes of fireworks were launched from 16 barges moored on the River Thames, turning the night sky into a spectacular light show.

MOST CANDLES ON A CAKE

The record for the most candles on a cake stands at 12,432 and was broken on 9 May 2003 in Ohio, USA – let's hope everyone's wishes came true!

LET'S GET THIS PARTY STARTED

These Guinness World Record holders really know how to party...

14 The maximum number of people (including the DJ!) who can fit into the Miniscule of Sound, the world's smallest nightclub

10,000 The number of people who can fit into Privilege in Ibiza, the world's largest nightclub

74 The number of hours that marathon DJ Martin Boss spun his wheels of steel to set the world's longest DJ session

13,588 The number of people dancing at the same time to the Village People's disco classic YMCA

QUIZ TIME On 13 June 2003, 645 people took part in the world's largest fight with which fluffy bedroom furnishing?

There's nothing more exciting than some VIP treatment at the world's most luxurious hotels. Imagine spending a night in some of these five-star record breakers...

glamorous

CHILLING OUT

You certainly won't need air conditioning if you're staying at the Ice Hotel in Jukkasjärvi, Sweden. This frozen retreat has 60 double rooms, 25 suites, a bar and a chapel... made entirely from ice!

DID YOU KNOW?

LARGEST PALACE

The Imperial Palace in Beijing, China, is the largest in the world. Known as the Summer Palace, it's so large you could fit over 240 jumbo jets inside it!

TALLEST HOTEL

Towering high over the sands just south of Dubai, United Arab Emirates, is the Burj Al Arab ('The Arabian Tower'). At over 320 m high, it's the perfect place for a girl to get away from it all and stick her head in the clouds.

QUIZ TIME Famous for its romantic capital city of Paris, which European country holds the record as the world's most popular tourist destination?

GET AWAY FROM IT ALL

Can't wait to go on holiday? There are so many fabulous choices for a girl these days. If you fancy a bit of history, then why not visit the world's oldest hotel, the Hoshi Ryokan in Awazu, Japan? It's 1,287 years old! If you're in a spending mood then jet over to Switzerland and book the Imperial Suite at the President Wilson Hotel in Geneva. But be ready to fork out – it's the world's most expensive hotel suite and will cost you SF45,000 (£20,907) a night!

DID YOU KNOW?

LARGEST HOTEL

The MGM Grand Hotel and Casino in Las Vegas, Nevada, USA, consists of four 30-storey towers. Inside are some 5,005 rooms, a massive concert arena and its very own theme park!

locations

LARGEST AREA OF POLISHED MARBLE

There's nothing like cool marble to give a place a bit of class, and the Venetian Resort-Hotel-Casino in Las Vegas has plenty of it. Its floors are plastered in 139,354 m^2 of the stuff – enough to cover 535 tennis courts.

HOW DOES YOU MEASURE UP?

Get yourself a map of the world and mark all the countries you've visited. Then, using the scale on the map, work out how far around the world you've travelled. Now compare it with Columbus, the world's most travelled teddy bear, who has visited 16 countries and covered some 330,000 Km.

QUIZ TIME The tallest pyramid in the world is the Great Pyramid of Khufu at Giza. n which African country can it be found?

LARGEST PIZZA

Ingredients:
4,500 kg flour • 180 kg margarine • 90 kg salt • 90 kg yeast • 2,925 litres water • 900 kg tomato puree • 900 kg chopped tomato • 800 kg mushrooms • 9 kg mixed herbs • 1,800 kg cheese

1. Combine the dough ingredients in an industrial mixer.
2. Roll out dough and top with tomatoes, cheese and mushrooms.
3. Place on a giant hotplate and heat with gas blowers from beneath. To cook the topping, suspend industrial burners from cranes over the pizza. Continue to cook... for 39 hours!

fantastic

This monster sculpture is actually made from popcorn! It's 4 m tall and took 630 hours to stick together. There's enough popcorn here to feed 2,400 hungry cinemagoers.

DID YOU KNOW?

MOST EXPENSIVE BURGER

In January 2003, a gourmet burger was added to the menu of DB Bistro Moderne in New York City, USA, costing a breath-taking $50 (£27.70). Not quite your average Big Mac!

QUIZ TIME True or false? The world's largest chocolate bar weighed the same as two fully grown cows.

Feeling peckish? Satisfy your cravings for something delicious with these tasty record-breaking treats.

food

COOKIE MONSTER

When one just isn't enough, dip into the world's largest bag of cookies. It was 3.29 m tall and contained 100,152 cookies – now, these should last a few days!

LARGEST MILKSHAKE

Thirsty? The world's largest milkshake should do the trick! This massive milkshake made in 2000 in New York, USA, contained nearly 23,000 litres of ice cream and milk. – enough for 50,000 regular-sized shakes (and enough to fill about 350 bath tubs!)

DID YOU KNOW?

STRAPPING STRAWBERRY

If fruit's your favourite, sink your teeth into the world's largest strawberry. This beast of a berry tipped the scales at 231 g – the weight of five golf balls!

* QUIZ TIME How much did six diners spend on one meal at the Petrus restaurant in London in 2001? a) £440 b) £4,400 c) £44,000

RECORD PROFILES

MARY-KATE & ASHLEY olsen

NAMES: Mary-Kate and Ashley Olsen
DATE OF BIRTH: 13 June 1986
PLACE OF BIRTH: Los Angeles, California, USA
OCCUPATION: Actresses

DID YOU KNOW?

EARLY START

The twins' first role was on the US sitcom Full House at the tender age of just nine months! Both girls played the same character, taking turns to appear on screen!

MARY-KATE & ASHLEY facts

- These high-flying twins share the record for the highest earnings for a TV child actor. At the age of nine, they were earning $79,000 (£56,000) for each episode of Full House.

- The Olsen girls have since shot to stardom and now have a TV series of their very own called So Little Time. They have also appeared in a several TV movies – and you can even buy Mary-Kate and Ashley dolls!

JK facts

- JK Rowling's Harry Potter books are so popular with both children and adults that she's quickly become the wealthiest author in the world, with a net worth of $1 billion (£548 million).
- The Harry Potter books also hold records for the fastest selling fiction book (Harry Potter and the Goblet of Fire), the best selling children's book series, as well as the largest first-edition print run.

DID YOU KNOW?

RICHER THAN ROYALTY

Rowling is the richest woman in the UK (yes, even richer than the Queen!), and one of five self-made female billionaires on the planet! To think that lots of publishers initially turned her down!

JK rowling

NAME: Joanne Kathleen Rowling

DATE OF BIRTH: 31 July 1965

PLACE OF BIRTH: Chipping Sodbury, UK

OCCUPATION: Children's author

GORGEOUS GORGE

Woah! Don't stand too close to the edge! The mighty Grand Canyon in Arizona, USA, is about 16 Km wide and up to 1.6 Km deep! It stretches for 446 Km – longer than the distance between London and Paris!

What an incredible world we live in! Check out some of the planet's most breathtaking natural wonders... you won't believe your eyes.

beautiful

DID YOU KNOW?

HIGHEST WATERFALL

The majestic Salto Angel waterfall in Venezuela is a truly breathtaking sight. The water plunges from a neck-craning height of 979 m – 10 times higher than the Statue of Liberty!

LARGEST EXPLORED UNDERWATER CAVE

Packed full of cool stalactites (they hang down) and stalagmites (they stick up), Nohoch Na Chich in Mexico stretches for over 70 km underground – and that's just the bits that have been measured!

HOW DO YOU MEASURE UP?

You might not find a pot of gold at the end of a rainbow, but you might find your name in the record books! The challenge is spotting the world's longest lasting rainbow. Using a stopwatch and a lot of patience, you'll need to find a rainbow that will last longer than the current record – a rainbow over Wetherby in the UK, lasted 6 hours!

QUIZ TIME The largest snowflake ever recorded fell on 28 January 1887 and was collected by rancher Matt Coleman. But how big was this flake? a) 4 cm b) 18 cm c) 38 cm

planet

SURF'S UP

Surf chicks – grab your board and ride the world's largest ever wave! Measured in February 1933, this towering wall of water was 34 m high from trough to crest. It was created during a hurricane that had wind speeds reaching 126 km/h.

TE-REEF-IC!

Home to hundreds of varieties of sealife, the Great Barrier Reef is the longest in the world, stretching for 2,027 Km along the northeast coast of Australia. Coral reefs are made up of billions of tiny living creatures, and this record-breaking structure took 600 million years to form.

DID YOU KNOW?

LARGEST ICEBERG

In November 1956, an iceberg was spotted in the South Pacific that was a little larger than usual – it was as big as Belgium! Just think of the number of drinks you could make with it.

QUIZ TIME The highest mountain in the world is 8,848 m high and is found in the Himalayan mountain range in Asia. What is this mountain called?

FASTEST CIRCUMNAVIGATION
Ellen MacArthur sailed around the globe in just 94 days 4 hr 25 min 40 sec during the 2000 Vendee Globe single-handed yacht race.

IN A SPIN

In April 2003, Swiss iceskater Lucinda Ruh managed a record-breaking 115 continuous spins while standing on one leg.

Sports aren't just for the boys – sporty girls are breaking records all over the world! Which of these fantastic feats would you like to break?

HOW DO YOU MEASURE UP?

Think you can run with the fastest women in the world? Then why not test yourself on the track? Find your local public athletics track and, with a friend timing you, see how close you can get to the 100 m world record. If it's not too far off Florence Griffith-Joyner's time of 10.49 seconds then maybe you should aim for a career in athletics!

QUIZ TIME The most Olympic gold medals won by a woman at one games was by German swimmer Kristin Otto at the 1988 games. How many did she win? a) 2 b) 4 c) 6

SUPER SPORTS

POMPOM POWER

There's more to cheerleading than just shaking your pompoms! A record-breaking group of 328 cheerleaders between the ages of 4 and 60 performed a cheer – in full uniform – in a football field in Kentucky, USA, on 20 October 2001.

DEEP-SEA DIVA

Good at holding your breath? Tanya Streeter of the USA certainly is! She holds the record for the deepest no-limits freedive, descending to a depth of 160 m on 17 August 2002 without using diving gear! Brave girl!

CHILL OUT

Yoga is all about stretching your body and clearing your mind. Sound like your idea of exercise? You would have loved taking part in the world's largest yoga class. This took place in February 2003 at Jabalpur, India – with 6,315 people!

DID YOU KNOW?

MAKING WAVES

The greatest distance covered by a woman in a 50-metre pool is 95.657 km! This breath-taking feat was achieved by Kelly Driffield of Australia in June 1997.

✱ QUIZ TIME The world's youngest gymnastics champion competing in beam, vault, floor and uneven bars is Aurelia Dobre from Romania. How old was she when she won the title? a) 8 b) 14 c)21

GIRLY GADGETS

Can you imagine a world without gadgets? No laptops, no email and worst of all, no mobiles! How did we communicate before txting?

ROBODOG

This cute little guy is Sony's AIBO, the world's fastest selling entertainment robot (AIBO means 'pal' in Japanese). Although he costs $2,066 (£1,132), the first 3,000 sold out in just 20 minutes! This robo-puppy can recognize its own name and surroundings, and can even learn to perform tricks.

TEXT MESSAGE CHALLENGE

Fast with your fingers? Then see if you can beat the Guinness World Record for texting. Type this message into your mobile in under 1 min 7 sec (without predictive text!): 'The razor-toothed piranhas of the genera Serrasalmus and Pygocentrus are the most ferocious freshwater fish in the world. In reality they seldom attack a human.'

QUIZ TIME Which country has the most telephones per person? a) UK b) USA c) Monaco

TALE OF THE MOBILE

Mobile phones aren't as modern as you think. Someone first had the idea over 50 years ago, although mobiles weren't actually available to us until the 1970s. The first ever call was made by the inventor Martin Cooper of Motorola on 3 April 1973, and the first mobile network was launched in Japan in 1979.

TITANIC TELEVISION

Not quite something for your bedroom, the world's largest TV set is the Sony JumboTron colour screen from Japan. It measured a whopping 24.3 m x 45.7 m – how cool would this look in your back garden?

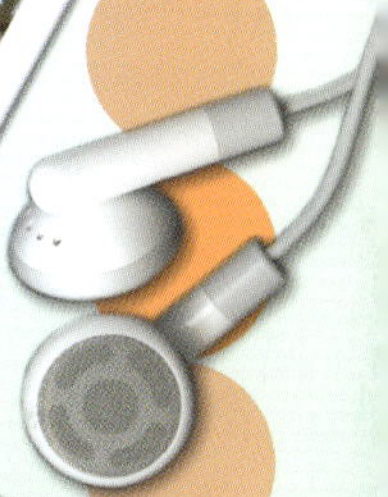

LITTLE WONDER

Tired of carrying around your heavy, clunky mobile? Yearning for something a little sleeker? Something a little more portable perhaps? Well, you'll love the Samsung SCH-M220 – it's just 92 mm long and 51 mm wide! Not only that, but it's even got a mini TV screen, so you'll never miss those important soaps again!

RING BLING

This sparkling mobile was designed by David Morris International to be the world's most expensive cellphone. Made from 18-carat gold, the keypad is covered with pink and white diamonds. The only snag is that it might be a little pricier than your usual pay-as-you-go set. It was sold in 1996 for a jaw-dropping £66,629 ($104,050)!

DID YOU KNOW?

THINNEST CAMERA

Able to fit into the smallest of handbags, the Ultra-Pocket digital camera is just 6 mm thick, weighs a mere 63.3 g and is the same size as a credit card!

QUIZ TIME Developed by the Sony Corporation in 1979, what's the world's most popular personal music system? a) Ghettoblaster b) Walkman c) iPod

DID YOU KNOW?

SCUBA DOOBY DO

Shadow the dog holds the record for the deepest canine scuba dive. Along with his owner, Dwane Folsom, Shadow regularly dives off the coast of Grand Cayman Island to depths of 4 m.

LONGEST EYELASHES

With lashes that would knock out a supermodel, Borders, a lhasa apso, has the longest eyelashes in the canine world, measuring 9 cm. Just imagine how much mascara she must get through!

perfect

PETITE PUP

The world's smallest dog is a tiny terrier named Tiny Pinocchio. At just 20.3 cm long and 12.06 cm tall, this dainty dog from Florida, USA, is not much bigger than a... hot dog

GO FETCH!

Augie the Golden Retriever holds the record for holding the most tennis balls in the mouth. He voluntarily chases after the balls and picks them up himself. At full stretch, he can cram in five – and he's still smiling!

CLEVER CANINE

Is your dog ultra-clever? Does it bow-wow you with hundreds of tricks? If so, see if your pup can beat record-holder Chanda-Leah, a toy poodle from Canada. She can perform 469 tricks, including playing the piano, barking her three, four and five times tables, and even riding a skateboard!

QUIZ TIME It's the canine version of the Oscars and it's held every year at the National Exhibition Centre in Birmingham, UK. But what is the name of the world's largest dog show?

pooches

They're loving, loyal and smart, so it's no surprise that record breaking comes easily to these dazzling dogs.

DID YOU KNOW?
DOG-EARED

A Basset Hound called Jack vom Forster Wald has ears that measure 33.2 cm from head to tip! What must it be like to have ears that touch the floor!?

HUGE HOUND

This dog really puts the 'great' into Great Dane! Harvey, from Marford, UK, is 105.4 cm tall and weighs 107 Kg. As big as a Shetland pony, he'd make a perfect guard dog. Harvey's so big that he's even got his own double bed to sleep in!

TOP DOG

Canine international superstar Jucki travels the globe competing in dog shows. She obviously has what it takes to be the best – since 1992, the glamorous German shepherd has won 'best in show' 67 times on five continents!

QUIZ TIME The richest dog in the world was a poodle named Toby. He was left the cash when his owner died in 1931, but how much did the lucky dog inherit? a) £150,000 b) £1.5 million c) £10.5 million

RECORD PROFILES

GUINNESS WORLD RECORDS

NAME: Venus Ebone Starr Williams
DATE OF BIRTH: 17 June 1980
PLACE OF BIRTH: California, USA
OCCUPATION: Professional tennis player

VENUS facts

- Venus is the professional powerhouse of the tennis world, blasting the fastest serve in the women's game. Opponents better watch out as she can fire a serve at 205 Km/h!
- She turned professional at the age of just 14, but continued to focus on her schoolwork for another two years before developing her tennis career.

DID YOU KNOW?

SIBLING RIVALRY

Venus isn't the only member of the Williams' family to shine on the tennis court. Her younger sister Serena has won tournaments at Wimbledon, the US Open and the French Open.

VENUS williams

PAULA radcliffe

NAME: Paula Jane Radcliffe
DATE OF BIRTH: 17 December 1973
PLACE OF BIRTH: Northwich, UK
OCCUPATION: Professional athlete

DID YOU KNOW?

FAST LEARNER

Paula studied French, German and Economics at university. On her application form, she wrote under hobbies: "Represented Britain at Athletics… Enjoy reading and listening to music"!

PAULA facts

- Paula's crowning moment came in the 2003 London marathon. Here, she shattered her previous world record, setting an amazing time of 2 hours 15 minutes and 25 seconds.
- Marathon running wasn't Paula's first choice of event. In the past, she has stuck to shorter distances, and holds the European 10,000 m title and the Commonwealth 5,000 m title.

At the Movies

Katharine Hepburn

AND THE OSCAR GOES TO...

The queen of the silver screen is American actress Katharine Hepburn (above). This haughty screen siren has won four Best Actress Oscars, more than any other woman in history. She's most famous for choosing roles that portray strong, independent women.

The only person to be nominated for an acting Oscar more times than Katharine Hepburn is Meryl Streep, with 13 nominations (but she only won twice). In high school, Meryl was a cheerleader and home-coming queen, and before she got her big break, she worked as a waitress.

Lights, camera, action! Settle back with some soda and popcorn as we take you on a star-studded cruise through the glitzy world of Hollywood and the silver screen.

WHO IS SHE? – Vijaya Nirmala from India
WHY IS SHE HERE? – This media mogul has directed more movies than any other woman, putting together 42 films in just over 30 years since her first in 1972.

QUIZ TIME You're never too young for a career on the silver screen! How old was Shirley Temple when she became the youngest number one box office star? a) 3 b) 7 c) 15

MAKING A SPLASH

Everyone Knows that a film needs a handsome leading man. And the movie Titanic got it spot on with dreamboat Leonardo DiCaprio. With this hunk behind it, it's not surprising that this flick was the first to take over $1 billion and went on to make a record $1.835 billion (£1.297 billion)!

LARGEST BOX OF POPCORN

Something to see you through the longest film is the largest box of popcorn, which took nearly six hours to fill. The only snag would have been trying to carry it into the cinema – it weighed a whopping 1.04 tonnes!

DID YOU KNOW?

ROARING SUCCESS

Disney's The Lion King tops the charts as the highest earning animated movie. In the big bucks stakes, Simba and the gang pulled in $777.9 million (£486 million) at the box office.

DID YOU KNOW?

FAMOUS FROCKS

On 18 March 1999, a record 56 Oscar dresses were sold at auction in New York, USA. All had been worn to the Academy Awards by divas such as Liz Taylor, Sharon Stone and Uma Thurman.

HOW DO YOU MEASURE UP?

Make sure you've got lots of soft cushions if you want to break the movie watching marathon record – oh, and plenty of films to watch as well. You'll need to rent more than 34 movies, making sure that they last longer than 66 hr 30 min – perfect for a night (or is that a weekend!?) in with your friends!

QUIZ TIME Disney/Pixar's movie *Finding Nemo* took a record $70 million (£43 million) in its opening weekend. What sort of animal is the film's unlikely hero?

LONGEST LEGS

Look at the pins on this gal! Sam Stacy from Doncaster, UK, has legs that would reach as far as some people's shoulders! When they were measured in 2001, they stretched for a total of 126.36 cm – and Sam was only 17 at the time. How long are they going to be when she stops growing!?

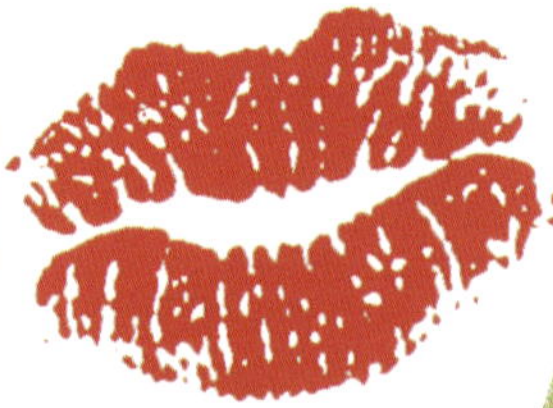

DID YOU KNOW?

LONGEST NECK

In parts of Burma, an extra long neck is a sign of beauty. Women of the Padaung and Kareni tribes use copper coils to stretch their necks, some up to 40 cm – the longest known in the world.

extreme

You can never spend too much time pampering yourself. But there are always a few girls who are ready to take beauty to a new level!

HOW DO YOU MEASURE UP?

Think you've got big hair? Then see if you can beat the record for the highest hairstyle. You'll need to backcomb all morning, as this record stands at 91.44 cm! It dates back to 18th-century France, when Queen Marie Antoinette had to have the highest hair in the land!

QUIZ TIME The largest global beauty pageant was the Miss World of 1999 held in London, UK. It was won by Yutka Mookhey from India. How many countries were represented? a) 12 b) 35 c) 94

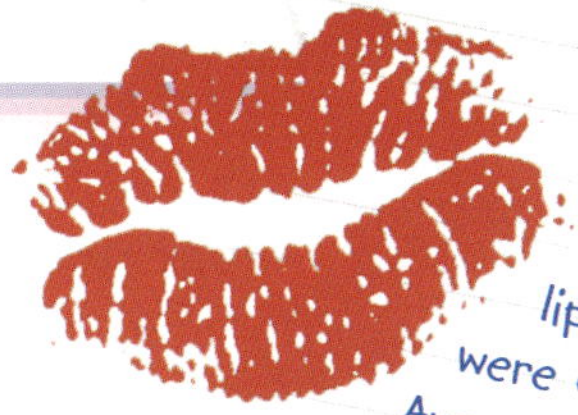

KISS COLLECTION

A total of 39,537 lipstick prints were collected by Avon Cosmetics in aid of the Kiss Goodbye to Breast Cancer campaign in 2001. Mwah!

beauty

HAIR RAISING

These brave volunteers are having their hair plaited together to create the world's longest braid! When it was completed, the braid measured 37.7 m using the hair from 65 girls.

DID YOU KNOW?

WHAT A WAIST!

Cathie Jung from the USA is 1.72 m tall but has the thinnest waist in the world. It measures just 38.1 cm – and she's not even breathing in!

QUIZ TIME True or false? Maria Rosa Abad of Spain set the record for the most rhinestones stuck to a body when she covered herself with 256 of these glittering jewels.

Rock and Pop

Westlife, Will Young, Robbie Williams... they're all record holders. Swooning yet? Slip on your headphones and read on.

DID YOU KNOW?
BIGGEST BAND
Far and away the biggest rock and pop band are The Beatles. Their record company EMI reckons they've sold over one billion discs and tapes so far!

IT'S A RAP
Hailing from Michigan, USA, Eminem smashed records in May 2002 when his album The Marshall Mathers LP sold 1.76 million copies in its first week, making the Slim Shady star the fastest selling rap artist in the world.

DID YOU KNOW?
WESTLIFE
The crooners from Ireland hold lots of records – not only have they had a total of 12 singles debut at No. 1 in the UK charts, but they made a record five public appearances in five cities in 36 hours!

QUIZ TIME The biggest selling single by a male solo artist is *Candle in the Wind 1997/Something About the Way You Look Tonight*. But which British singer recorded this song about Princess Diana?

MUSIC BY NUMBERS

134 The number of combined weeks that nine singles by Oasis spent in the UK singles chart in 1996 – a record for one year.

13 million The number of copies sold of Millennium by the Backstreet Boys – a record for a boyband.

$647 million The total wealth of the Rolling Stones, the world's wealthiest band.

DID YOU KNOW?

ROBBIE WILLIAMS

The cheeky former Take That star holds the record for the best album start by a UK solo artist. His first five albums, released between September 1997 and November 2002, have all made it to No. 1!

WHO IS HE? – Will Young
WHY IS HE HERE? – He holds the record for the biggest first week in the charts, selling 1,108,269 of his single Anything is Possible/Evergreen.

THE WILL YOUNG STORY

Born on 20 January 1979, the gorgeous Will Young grew up in the town of Hungerford in sleepy Berkshire, UK. But his quiet life came to an end when he became the first ever winner of Pop Idol in 2002, beating other hopeful Gareth Gates in the final. Will won the hearts of the nation when he famously took on evil judge Simon Cowell, and has since proved him wrong by becoming a regular UK chart topper.

MTV

MUSIC TELEVISION®

Beamed live into 281.7 million homes in 79 countries around the world, MTV is the world's largest music station. It's so big that it can be seen by one quarter of the world's total TV audience!

QUIZ TIME Rod Stewart holds the record for the largest free rock concert attendance. But how many people were in the crowd at the gig on New Year's Eve 1994? a) 350,000 b) 3.5 million c) 35 million

Weddings

Wedding

YOU ARE CORDIALLY INVITED TO THE MARRIAGE **again!** OF DAVID AND LAUREN

OOPS, I DID IT AGAIN!

Lauren and David Blair from the USA have reaffirmed their vows a total of 66 times since they got married in 1984!

LONGEST WEDDING BOUQUET

This brill bouquet was made for a wedding in Lisbon, Portugal, in 2002. Made up of roses, orchids, asparagus stems and beargrass, it was 42 m long and weighed 60 Kg! Fátima Fernandes was the blushing bride who had to carry it, but who was the lucky girl who caught it at the end?

DID YOU KNOW?

OLDEST BRIDE

It's never too late, as Minnie Munro from Australia proved when she married her toyboy Dudley Read in 1991. He was 83, and she was 102!

QUIZ TIME Octavio Guillan and Adriana Martinez finally married each other when they were aged 82. How long did their engagement last? a) 6 years b) 25 years c) 67 years

Here comes the bride! And all of these ladies have found record-breaking ways of getting to the altar – and some of them can't seem to stay away!

ROYAL ROMANCE

When Lady Diana Spencer married HRH Prince Charles on 29 July 1981, it was watched on TV by an estimated 750 million people in 74 countries – the largest ever TV audience for a wedding!

DID YOU KNOW?

MAKE UP YOUR OWN MIND

Since 1957, Linda Essex from the USA has been married 23 times to 15 different men! Her last husband was Glynn 'Scotty' Wolfe, who holds the record for the most marriages by a male!

HOW DO YOU MEASURE UP?

Can't wait to marry Prince Charming? Every girl knows that you have to catch a bouquet first, so improve your chances and catch more than any other girl! Stephanie Monyak from Pennsylvania, USA, has caught a total of nine bridal bouquets that were tossed at weddings she has attended since 1983. Surely you can catch at least 10!

HOW DEEP IS YOUR LOVE?

Thinking of something a little different for your nuptials? Then how about holding it at sea? Or rather under the sea. That's what Toni Wilson and John Santino did in 2003, when 105 divers witnessed their wedding, setting the record for the largest underwater wedding!

QUIZ TIME Jane Williams and Debbie-Jane Hunt share the record for having the most bridesmaids t their weddings. How many do you think they each had? a) 3 b) 12 c) 28

RECORD PROFILES

DID YOU KNOW?

AWESOME AUDIENCE

Since making her TV debut aged just 11, Charlotte has performed all around the globe in front of some of the world's most important people, including the President of the USA and the Pope!

CHARLOTTE church

NAME: Charlotte Church

DATE OF BIRTH: 21 February 1986

PLACE OF BIRTH: Cardiff, Wales, UK

OCCUPATION: Singer

CHARLOTTE facts

- The warbler from Wales is the world's youngest person to top the classical charts.
- Her album, Voice of an Angel, went double platinum in just four weeks!
- Charlotte recently turned 18, which meant she could get her hands on her enormous £16.4 million fortune... but she insists she won't go on a massive spending spree!

DID YOU KNOW?

FRIENDS FACTFILE

The wardrobe department has an entire room just for handbags • 32 pots of coffee are drunk during the filming of each show • Phoebe has sung 25 original songs since the start of the show.

FRIENDS facts

- The girls from Friends hold the record for the highest earnings for a TV actress. Each of them takes home an amazing $1 million (£703,334) for each show!
- Many girls reckon that Jennifer is the luckiest girl in the world – she's married to heart-throb Brad Pitt!!!
- Courteney met her movie-star husband David Arquette on the set of Scream.

FRIENDS

NAME: Courteney Cox Arquette
DATE OF BIRTH: 15 June 1964
PLACE OF BIRTH: Alabama, USA
OCCUPATION: Actress

NAME: Lisa Kudrow
DATE OF BIRTH: 30 July 1963
PLACE OF BIRTH: California, USA
OCCUPATION: Actress

NAME: Jennifer Aniston
DATE OF BIRTH: 11 February 1969
PLACE OF BIRTH: California, USA
OCCUPATION: Actress

Whether it's a jaunt to Gibraltar or a vacation in Venice, there is no excuse for not travelling in style.

LUXURY

DID YOU KNOW?

HOT WHEELS

The Mazda MX-5 Miata is the world's best selling two-seater sports car. This nippy little runabout sold 600,000 units between its launch in April 1989 and April 2001.

FIT FOR A QUEEN

The Cunard Line's Queen Mary 2 made its maiden voyage in January 2004. It three times larger than Titanic and has space for 2,620 passengers and 1,253 crew. It's also the first ship to have its own planetarium!

QUIZ TIME Hollywood actress Ginger Rogers holds the record for the largest travelling wardrobe. But how many pieces of luggage did she bring with her from America in 1969? a) 3 b) 45 c) 118

TRAVEL

LENGTHY LIMO

Girls will go to any lengths for a bit of comfort. This super-stretch limo is 30.5 m long and includes luxuries such as a swimming pool with diving board, a water bed and even a helicopter pad!

SUPERSONIC

When you've got a shopping trip planned in New York City, the sooner you get there the better. What you need is an aeroplane that can go faster than the speed of sound! That's exactly what Concorde could do, the holder of the fastest trans-Atlantic flight. On 7 February 1996, it crossed the pond in 2 hr 52 min 59 sec, breaking its own record by 1 min 30 secs – and all in the lap of luxury, naturally.

DID YOU KNOW?

COSMOPOLITAN CAT

Smarty is a well-travelled feline – he holds the record for the most air flights made by a domestic cat! This pampered puss has flown 74 times between Cairo and Larnaca, Cyprus!

JOIN THE JET SET

Fancy a little day trip to your villa in the south of France? Then you simply must travel in style in your own private jet. A Gulfstream V-SP is the best that money can buy – at $45 million (£31 million) you're guaranteed to fly first class!

SAIL OF THE CENTURY

Imagine stretching out on the deck of your own record-breaking yacht as it speeds through the ocean! The largest yacht in the world is 147 m long and belongs to the Saudi Arabian royal family. Built in Denmark, it was estimated to be worth over $100 million (£63 million)! Now that's luxury!

QUIZ TIME True or false? The Sultan of Brunei has the biggest private collection of Rolls Royces with 150.

DONKEY'S YEARS

Born in 1948, Suzy the donkey from the Moon Ranch in New Mexico, USA, is twice as old as the average donkey. She'll celebrate her 57th birthday in 2005, making her the oldest living donkey in the world.

DID YOU KNOW?

HIGH FLYING HORSE

One horse with its head in the clouds is Optibeurs Leonardo. Ridden by Franke Sloothaak from Germany, this horsey high jumper cleared 2.4 m in 1991!

Horses

HUGE HORSE

The tallest horse in the world is a giant stallion from Texas, USA, called Prince Jordan of Lakeview. Known as Goliath, this majestic horse stands 195.58 cm tall, and everyday eats 22.6 kg hay and drinks 113.5 litres of water!

QUIZ TIME True or false? Old Billy, the world's oldest ever horse, lived to be 103 years old.

LARGEST EQUESTRIAN EVENT

A total of 162 expert riders from 37 different countries gathered on 10 December 1998 at the elite Ghantoot Race Club in the United Arab Emirates. The riders set off on a 160-km desert trek as part of the International Equestrian Federation's World Endurance Championships, and the race was won by America's Valerie Kanavy.

PRICEY PONY

The most valuable horse in the world is a six-year-old broodmare from Kentucky, USA, called Cash Run. She came from a family of top stallions and was purchased for $7,100,000 (£4,186,814) on 3 November 2003.

Woah there! Grab your riding boots and jodhpurs and hold your reins tight. We're off on a gallop through a fab collection of riding records!

& ponies

MINIATURE MARE

Let's give a big hand to the world's smallest horse. Black Beauty, a miniature black mare born in 1997, is not much taller than your knee! Even when this fun-sized foal grew up she weighed just 18.8 kg and measured a mere 47 cm to the top of her shoulder – that's about the same size as a cocker spaniel!

HOW DO YOU MEASURE UP?

You may not own a real horse yet, but it doesn't mean you can't be a rodeo queen! Britain's Pauline Farrington was able to set mechanical rodeo record when she held on to the bucking bronco for 58.1 seconds in September 2000. Could you do better?

QUIZ TIME Held on 31 July 1999 in the Colombian city of Medellín, the world's largest horse parade featured how many horses? a) 25 b) 276 c) 7,895

FANTASTICALLY FLOPPY-EARED

You can say that again! The rabbit with the longest ears is an English Lop called Nipper's Geronimo. Each of Nipper's ears is longer than your arm, and together they reach an incredible 79 cm! The tortoise-shell buck is owned by Waymon and Margaret Nipper of Bakersfield, California, USA.

DID YOU KNOW?

HUGE HAMSTER FAMILY

A hamster belonging to the Miller family of Louisiana, USA, gave birth to a litter of 26 baby hamsters! The average number is 8 babies per litter!

GROWING OLD GRACEFULLY

Guinea pigs usually live to be five years old, but not Snowball. This geriatric guinea pig lived to the grand old age of 14 years 10 months!

HOW DO YOU MEASURE UP?

Have you got a record-breaking pet? Before Guinness World Records can accept your claim, you need to ask your vet to provide all the information we need – length, height, weight and age. Make sure your pet is fully grown before you write to us – and PLEASE don't force feed your pet to make it fat! We think this is cruel so we won't accept claims for heaviest pet! Good luck!

FORMULA ONE FERRETS

You've heard of greyhound racing and horse racing... but have you ever heard of ferret racing? It's true! In July 1999, 150 ferrets took part in the North England Ferret Racing Championships. The 10-metre race was won by a fiery ferret called Warhol, who finished in a spectacular 12.59 seconds!

QUIZ TIME True or false? The smallest breed of rabbit is the Polish dwarf, which weighs just 5.4 kg.

From long-eared lops to super-fast ferrets, here are a few impressive pets that any girl would be proud to call her own.

DID YOU KNOW?

BLABBERMOUTH BUDGIE

Puck the budgie from California, USA, was never short for words! This babbling budgie had the largest vocabulary of any bird – he was able to squawk out 1,728 different words!

pets

PLUCKY PARROT

During Christmas 1999 a fire broke out in the home of Charlie the parrot in Durham, UK. He squawked so loudly that he woke up his owner and her five children, who all escaped from the flames. Sadly, Charlie was not so fortunate.

ROMANTIC RODENT

Sooty from South Wales holds the record for the most Valentines cards received by a guinea pig! He was sent 206 cards – some from as far away as New Zealand – after he managed to father 43 babies by 24 partners in a single night!

QUIZ TIME Puckel Martin holds the record for the highest jump by a guinea pig. How high did Puckel jump in March 2003? a) 2 cm b) 20 cm c) 200 cm

PLANTS AND FLOWERS

Step into your very own enchanted garden with these fruity, fragrant records.

FLORAL TRIBUTE

Following the death of Princess Diana in 1997, an estimated 10,000–15,000 tonnes of flowers were laid outside Kensington Palace, London, in her memory, creating the world's largest floral tribute.

WHAT IS IT? – Hampton Court Maze, UK
WHY IS IT HERE? – One place you can really lose yourself, it was designed in 1690 and is the oldest hedge maze in the world.

HOW DO YOU MEASURE UP

TRY YOUR HAND AT THESE FLOWER ARRANGING RECORDS:

- Largest floral arrangement with most different types of flowers. You will need: more than 1,010 different types of flowers, some water, a very big vase
- Tallest flower arrangement: You will need: more than 33,350 carnations, some water, another very big vase. Oh, and your arrangement will need to be over 16 metres high!

QUIZ TIME The sunflower with the most heads on it was grown by Melvin Hemker of the USA in 2001. How many flowers did it have? a) 2 b) 25 c) 837

FABULOUS FRUIT

- Alan Smith of Kent, UK, grew the world's biggest apple in October 1997. It weighed in at a whopping 1.67 kg!
- And how about this for a peach of a record? In September 2000, Steve Lubisich from California, USA, grew a 'Snow Giant' peach that tipped the scales at 680 g!
- Have you heard on the grapevine about the world's biggest bunch of grapes? A company in Chile in South America grew a bunch that weighed 9.4 kg!

DID YOU KNOW?

FLOWER POWER

Imagine the fragrance in the air at the Roseto di Cavriglia in Cavrigalia, Italy. It's the world's largest rose garden, with over 7,500 different varieties of rose!

FIT FOR A KING

The largest garden in the world was created in the 17th century for the French King Louis XIV at the Palace of Versailles, just outside Paris. The garden has 200,000 trees and 50 fountains (including some that play music) and 210,000 new flowers are planted every year.

QUIZ TIME Which bendy, yellow-coloured fruit is the most consumed fruit in the world?

LONGEST CAT
Leo, a Maine Coon cat from the USA, measures a mog-nificent 122 cm from the tip of his nose to the tip of his tail! Leo's real name is almost as long as his body – it's Verismo's Leonetti Reserve Red – and his favourite food is blue cheese.

DID YOU KNOW?
FILTHY RICH FELINE
Blackie the cat inherited a cool $21.6 million (£12 million) as specified in the will of his doting millionaire owner Ben Rea. Only in America!

cool prrrrrrrrrrrrfect!

From your pet tabby cat to a majestic big cat in the wild, our furry feline friends are fantastic at breaking records.

HOW DOES YOUR CAT MEASURE UP?
One of the most popular claims submitted to Guinness World Records is for the cat with most toes. Do you think your kitty has a record-breaking number of digits? If so, he or she needs to have more toes than Jake the ginger tabby, who has 28 in total – seven on each paw!

MOST TRAVELLED TABBY
In February 1984, a cat named Hamlet escaped from his cage on a flight out of Toronto, Canada. He got trapped behind some airplane panelling for over seven weeks and accidentally travelled nearly 960,000 km through the air!

QUIZ TIME Capable of running at speeds of about 100 km/h, this fast feline is the quickest land mammal on the planet. Can you name it?

cats

CUTE CUBS

Six cuddly Bengal white tiger cubs were born in Buenos Aires Zoo, Argentina, in November 2003. These adorable white cubs with blue eye and chocolate brown stripes make the record books as the largest litter of tigers ever born in captivity.

OLDEST CAT

Two geriatric moggies share the record for the world's oldest cat. Granpa Rex Allen, a show cat from Austin, Texas, and Ma, a feline tabby from Devon, UK, both lived to the ripe old age of 34!

WORLD'S LARGEST FELINE

Don't stand too close to this kitty! The beautiful Siberian tiger is the ruler of the feline world, weighing in at an amazing 265 kg (that's about the weight of four human adults!). These endangered big cats eat about 45 kg of meat (that's probably as heavy as you!) in one go!

DID YOU KNOW?

TREMENDOUS TAIL

On 21 March 2001, when Furball the cat from Michigan, USA, had his tail measured, he got his name into the record books. It stretched for an amazing 40.6 cm!

QUIZ TIME Towser the female tortoiseshell cat holds the record for catching more mice than any other cat. How many mice did the great mouser catch in her lifetime? a) 363 b) 8,274 c) 28,899

RECORD • PROFILES • GUINNESS WORLD RECORDS

NAME: Kylie Ann Minogue

DATE OF BIRTH: 28 May 1968

PLACE OF BIRTH: Melbourne, Victoria, USA

OCCUPATION: Actress, singer

KYLIE facts

- The pint-sized performer from down under holds the record for being the biggest pop earner from Australia. During a 16-date tour in 2001, Kylie sold 200,000 tickets for the shows and earned a very nice $5 million.

- As well as singing, Kylie has turned her hand at acting, appearing in screen soaps Skyways, The Sullivans, The Henderson Kids and Neighbours as well as the movies Street Fighter and The Delinquents.

DID YOU KNOW?

FILM FAIRY

One of Kylie's latest screen appearances was as a small green fairy in Baz Luhrmann's Moulin Rouge.

DID YOU KNOW?

JUNK FOOD DISCOVERY

Gisele was first spotted by modelling scouts while she was tucking into a burger in a McDonalds' in Sao Paulo. She moved away from home straight away to start her modelling career, aged just 14 .

NAME: Gisele Bündchen

DATE OF BIRTH: 20 July 1980

PLACE OF BIRTH: Horizonta, Rio Grande do Sul, Brazil

OCCUPATION: Model

GISELE facts

- Topping the supermodel charts, Gisele earnt more than any other catwalk queen in 2001. In that year, she collected a cool $12.5 million (£8.3 million) for her modelling work – nice job if you can get it. And she got to date Leonardo DiCaprio!
- During her career, she's modelled for all of the biggest names in the fashion world – Ralph Lauren, Valentino, Versace, Dolce & Gabbana; it reads like our dream wardrobe!

Kings

All girls dream of the royal life and living happily ever after. These record-breaking royals prove that it's possible...

DID YOU KNOW?

YOUNGEST QUEEN

This stunning beauty just so happens to be the world's youngest current queen. She's Queen Rania Al-Abdullah of Jordan and her husband was crowned in 1993 when she was just 28 years 160 days old.

TALLEST CROWN PRINCE

Principe de Asturias, Don Felipe be Borbón y Grecia (catchy title, that one) stands tall at a skyscraping 1.97 m. He's the son of King Juan Carlos of Spain.

TALE OF A PRINCESS

Once upon a time there was a maid who lost her glass slipper at a ball and later became a princess. The story of Cinderella has been told on screen more times than any other. To date, there's been 98 productions in total, including ballets, operas and Disney's cartoon version, as well as parodies.

QUIZ TIME True or false? Gianni Versace designed a diamond-studded tiara costing £3.2 million.

& Queens

DID YOU KNOW?

HEAVYWEIGHT KING

Tipping the scales as the world's heaviest monarch is King Taufa'ahau Tupou IV of Tonga. When he was weighed in September 1976 he came in at a whopping 209.5 kg!

LONGEST REIGNING ROYAL

No living queen has reigned longer than Her Majesty Queen Elizabeth II of the UK and Commonwealth, who took to the throne on 6 February 1952. She celebrated her Golden Jubilee in 2002.

Royal hunk Prince William has more fan clubs devoted to him than any other royal in the world. At the last count, there were at least 48 clubs dedicated to Britain's future King can we join them all?

QUIZ TIME Which royal residence in Berkshire, UK, is the world's largest inhabited castle? a) Buckingham Palace b) Windsor Castle c) Hampton Court Palace

LONG LEGS

These giant jeans were made by Levi Strauss Co, Inc. of Canada. They are the largest ever made, and are 28.6 m long and nearly 19 m wide – that's bigger than a house!

Fashion rules – it's something that every girl knows. So break out your glammest frocks and read all about the coolest records on the catwalk.

fabulous

DID YOU KNOW?

RICHEST SUPERMODEL

Although she no longer struts her stuff on the catwalk, Elle MacPherson, aka 'The Body', is said to be worth £23 million.

FASHION FIGURES

1921 The year in which fashion designer Gabrielle (Coco) Chanel launched Chanel No. 5, the first perfume by a couturier.

121 The length in metres of the world's longest sari.

114.4 The record-breaking distance in kilometres walked on a catwalk by models Roberta Brown and Lorraine McCourt.

QUIZ TIME Claudia Schiffer has appeared on more magazine covers than any other supermodel. But how many? a) over 20 b) over 150 c) over 500

fashion

HOW DO YOU MEASURE UP?

A girl can never have too many clothes. Wouldn't it be great to have all the money in the world to spend on our wardrobes?

- $1,267,000 (£767,042): Most expensive dress (worn by Marilyn Monroe)
- $46,532 (£33,039): Most valuable pair of jeans (a 120-year-old pair of Levi's)
- $101,500 (£70,894): Most expensive antique dress – a court-dress dating from 1888
- $85,000 (£48,571): Pearl-studded shoes from the House of Berluti, Paris

DID YOU KNOW?

HEAD IN THE CLOUDS

If you like tottering down the road in killer heels then these are the shoes for you. Made by LadyBWear, the Vertigo shoes have a heel measuring a head-spinning 41 cm!

HUMUNGOUS HANDBAG

Now here's something that should just about fit all our shopping. Made in Brazil, it's the world's largest handbag, measuring 3.7 m tall and 3.54 m wide! It's way too big to carry around – but we can dream can't we?

QUIZ TIME Ginger Spice, aka Geri Halliwell, wore an outfit that became the world's most expensive tem of pop clothing. But how much did her mini Union Jack dress sell for? a) $12 b) $2,356 c) $66,112

Nations

Globetrotting girls know that records are set all around the world... you just have to know where to look!

DID YOU KNOW?
PET POLITICS

US President Bill Clinton adopted a cat named Socks in 1991. When he moved into the White House, Socks received 75,000 letters and parcels every week, making him the world's most popular political cat.

USA: In 2000, Americans were the most frequent fliers, covering 1,110.8 billion km

Mexico: home to the Ramos Gomez family, the hairiest in the world

Brazil: Tião the chimpanzee won 400,000 votes when he stood in a mayoral election in Rio de Janeiro in 1988 – the most votes for a chimp!

KIDS GALORE

The Pacific paradise of the Marshall Islands is home to the largest population of children in the world. In July 2001, census figures showed that 49.29% of the population were under the age of 15.

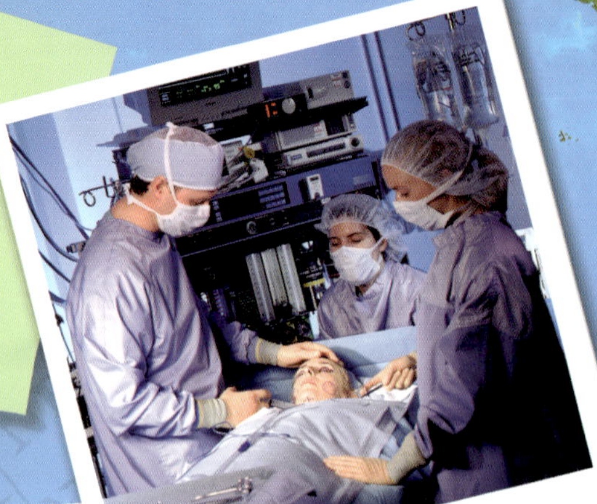

NIP AND TUCK

The country with the most plastic surgeons is the USA – in fact, it's got almost half of the world's nip-and-tuck specialists. The US city with the most surgeons is New York, although there are more per capita in San Francisco.

New Zealand: the first nation to grant women the right to vote in 1893

Andes: The longest mountain range stretches through seven countries for 7,600 km

QUIZ TIME The country with the shortest life expectancy is the African nation of Sierra Leone. What is the average life expectancy for women in this country? a) 24.5 years b) 39.8 years c) 72.5 years

of the World

Sweden: Country with most women ministers – with 11 ministers in a 22-strong cabinet

Ukraine: Largest shortage of men – with a female population of 53.7%

United Arab Emirates: Largest shortage of women – with a female population of just 32.46%

DID YOU KNOW?
PEOPLE EVERYWHERE

China boasts the largest population in the world with an estimated 1,286,975,468 in 2003 – and it's rising. Every year, this figure grows by about 16 million!

Japan: Longest life expectancy – women live to the ripe old age of 83.9 year (but men can only manage to reach 77.3!)

Niger: Country with the highest birth rate, with 52 births per 1,000 people (twice the world average)

Kerala, India: Largest annual gathering of women – 1.5 million women meet at the 'Pongala' religious offering

TOP LADY

Graca Machel holds the honour of being First Lady of more countries than any other woman. She was first married to the President of Mozambique and then to Nelson Mandela when he was President of South Africa.

THE WORLD IN FIGURES

11 The number of official languages of South Africa, the country with the most languages. They include Afrikaans, English and Swazi.

80,000 The number of people living on Ap Lei Chau, the world's most densely populated island. This island off Hong Kong is just 1.3 Km² so each person gets the equivalent of just 1.6 mm² of land!

530,773 The number of people involved in the largest simultaneous lesson, held in 32 countries on 9 April 2003.

QUIZ TIME Which North American country earns more than $85 billion from tourism every year, the world's highest?

How to set or break a Guinness World Record

1 If you want to set a brand new world record – or break an existing one – tell us first by visiting the "Be A Record Breaker" section of our website (address above).

2 Tell us as much as you can about your proposal. It takes about 10 weeks for us to process your application, so apply in plenty of time.

3 We'll write back to you and tell you whether or not we like your idea. If we think it's a good idea, we'll also send you the rules and guidelines you'll need to follow in order to attempt the record fairly and safely.

4 You can now attempt your record. We can't send adjudicators to every attempt, so we ask you to collect evidence of your claim. We ask for at least two signed witness statements, video footage and photographs.

5 Send us your evidence and we'll then investigate your claim fully. If you're successful, congratulations: you'll receive your official Guinness World Records certificate in the post!

Z ANSWERS

China
c
– Green
– Oyster
– a
– True. Her baby boy weighed
8 kg (23 lb 12 ozs).
– Australia. They eat 16.6 litres of ice
am per year each.
– 206.6 seconds
– Rio de Janeiro, Brazil, and
ıdon, UK
– Pillows
– France
– Egypt
– False. It weighed 2,280 kg – about as
ıvy as four cows.
– c
– c
– Mount Everest
– c
– b
– c
– b
– Crufts
– c

36 – b
37 – Clownfish
38 – c
39 – False. She covered her body in 30,361 rhinestones on 22 November 2001.
40 – Elton John. It sold 33 million copies in over 40 countries.
41 – b. It was held at Copacabana Beach, Rio de Janeiro, Brazil.
42 – c
43 – c
46 – c
47 – True
48 – False. He lived to be 63 years old.
49 – c
50 – False. It weighs less than 1.13 kg.
51 – b
52 – c
53 – Banana
54 – Cheetah
55 – c
58 – True
59 – b
60 – c
61 – c
62 – b
63 – USA